WOULD YOU RATHER

THE FAMILY FRIENDLY BOOK OF STUPIDLY SILLY,
CHALLENGING AND ABSOLUTELY HILARIOUS
QUESTIONS FOR KIDS, TEENS AND ADULTS
(FAMILY GAME BOOK GIFT IDEAS)

AMAZING ACTIVITY PRESS

WOULD YOU RATHER...

MOVE TO ANOTHER COUNTRY

- OR -

LIVE WHERE YOU ARE FOREVER?

GO TO SCHOOL IN THE CAR WITH YOUR MOM
AND DAD
- OR -
GO TO SCHOOL WITH YOUR FRIEND ON THE
PUBLIC BUS?

WOULD YOU RATHER...

BLOW A BALLOON TILL IT POPS

- *OR* -

POP A BALLOON WITH SOMETHING SHARP?

BE IN A DANCE CLASS

- *OR* -

BE IN THE CHOIR?

WOULD YOU RATHER...

HAVE NOISY FRIENDS

- OR -

HAVE NOSEY FRIENDS?

HAVE ONLY MULTICOLORED CLOTHES

- OR -

HAVE ONLY WHITE CLOTHES?

WOULD YOU RATHER...

LIVE WITH GRANDMA

- OR -

LIVE WITH YOUR COUSINS?

DRINK CHOCOLATE MILK

- OR -

DRINK HOT CHOCOLATE?

WOULD YOU RATHER...

GET ASSIGNMENTS EVERY SINGLE DAY FOR A YEAR

- OR -

BE STUCK IN SCHOOL FOR A YEAR?

HAVE NO NOSE AT ALL

- OR -

HAVE A NOSE AS LONG AS PINOCCHIO'S?

WOULD YOU RATHER...

STAIN YOUR MOUTH WITH CHICKEN SAUCE AND NOT KNOW

- *OR* -

STAIN YOUR HANDS WITH CHICKEN SAUCE AND NOT HAVE ANYTHING TO CLEAN IT WITH?

LOSE ALL YOUR BABY PICTURES

- *OR* -

LOSE ALL THE PICTURES FROM YOUR LAST BIRTHDAY?

WOULD YOU RATHER...

HAVE A BABY PEE ON YOU

- OR -

HAVE A BABY THROW UP ON YOU?

HAVE REALLY LONG TOENAILS
- OR -
HAVE REALLY LONG FINGERNAILS?

WOULD YOU RATHER...

HAVE A CHICKEN LAY EGGS IN YOUR HAIR

- OR -

HAVE A BIRD MAKE A NEST IN YOUR HAIR?

TRAVEL BY AIRPLANE

- OR -

TRAVEL BY HOT AIR BALLOON?

WOULD YOU RATHER...

LIVE ON A HOUSEBOAT

- OR -

LIVE IN A TREE HOUSE?

BE PRANKED

- OR -

BE A WELL-KNOWN PRANKSTER?

WOULD YOU RATHER...

HAVE TO POOP EVERY HOUR

- OR -

HAVE TO PEE EVERY HOUR?

HAVE YOUR OWN A JETPACK

- OR -

HAVE YOUR OWN ROBOT?

WOULD YOU RATHER...

RIDE THE BENCH ON A SPORTS TEAM THAT ALWAYS WINS

- OR -

BE THE STAR PLAYER ON A LOSING SPORTS TEAM AT SCHOOL?

GIVE YOUR ALREADY CHEWED GUM TO SOMEONE ELSE

- OR -

EAT A PIECE OF GUM FROM THE STREET?

WOULD YOU RATHER...

BE STUCK WITH A CLOWN THAT'S QUITE ANNOYING

- *OR* -

BE STUCK IN A ROOM WITH A CLOWN THAT'S NOT FUNNY?

A MAGIC WIZARD
- *OR* -
BE A SUPERHERO?

WOULD YOU RATHER...

HAVE THE POWER TO TRANSFORM INTO A BUTTERFLY

- *OR* -

TO TRANSFORM INTO AN EAGLE?

GET COTTON CANDY
- *OR* -
ICE-CREAM AT A PARK?

WOULD YOU RATHER...

MEET A CLOWN

- OR -

BE A CLOWN?

HAVE BADLY TRIMMED HAIR

- OR -

HAVE SMELLY HAIR?

WOULD YOU RATHER...

EAT FISH THAT'S HALF BURNT

- OR -

EAT FISH THAT'S HALF DONE?

HAVE CLAWS AS HANDS

- OR -

HOOKS AS A HAND?

WOULD YOU RATHER...

HAVE THE BUTTON ON YOUR JEANS FALL OFF

- OR -

HAVE THE ZIP OF YOUR JEANS CUT?

TAKE A DAY TRIP TO THE BEACH

- OR -

TAKE A DAY TRIP TO THE ZOO?

WOULD YOU RATHER...

BE THE 1ST FASTEST SWIMMER IN THE WORLD

- OR -

THE 2ND FASTEST RUNNER IN THE WORLD?

BE SUPERMAN'S SIDEKICK

- OR -

BE SPIDERMAN'S SIDEKICK?

WOULD YOU RATHER...

HAVE A HUNDRED MILLION DOLLARS WORTH
OF CANDY

- *OR* -

HAVE A MILLION DOLLARS IN PENNIES?

HAVE MILK RUN DOWN YOUR NOSE EVERY
TIME YOU LAUGH
- *OR* -
HAVE MILK RUN OUT OF YOUR EYES EVERY
TIME YOU CRIED?

WOULD YOU RATHER...

YOUR HANDS GOT DIRTY ALL THE TIME

- OR -

YOUR FEET GOT DIRTY ALL THE TIME?

RIDE ON A LION

- OR -

RIDE ON THE BACK OF A TIGER?

WOULD YOU RATHER...

WAKE UP WITH WINGS

- OR -

WAKE UP WITH A TAIL?

WEAR TRENDY SNEAKERS

- OR -

WEAR CUTE SHOES?

WOULD YOU RATHER...

BE A PART OF A CIRCUS SHOW

- OR -

GO WATCH A CIRCUS SHOW?

LIVE IN A CAVE ALONE

- OR -

LIVE IN A CAVE WITH A FRIENDLY BEAR?

WOULD YOU RATHER...

HAVE A HOLE IN YOUR OUTFIT AND NOT NOTICE

- OR -

HAVE A STAIN ON YOUR OUTFIT AND NOT NOTICE?

MAKE BURPS THAT SMELL REALLY BAD
- OR -
MAKE LOUD BURPS THAT ARE HARD TO IGNORE?

WOULD YOU RATHER...

GO OUTSIDE AND PLAY WITH YOUR FRIENDS

- OR -

HAVE YOUR FRIENDS COME OVER?

MEET A FAIRY

- OR -

A GODDESS?

WOULD YOU RATHER...

WEAR DORA THE EXPLORER PAJAMAS

- *OR* -

WEAR SPONGEBOB PAJAMAS?

SHARE YOUR BED WITH SOMEONE WHO FARTS
A LOT
- *OR* -
SHARE YOUR BED WITH SOMEONE WHO PEES
ON THE BED?

WOULD YOU RATHER...

PLAY GAMES ON A PHONE

- *OR* -

PLAY A BOARD GAME?

BE THE HEAD OF THE FBI FOR THE PRESIDENT

- *OR* -

BE A SUPERHERO THAT NEVER GAINS
RECOGNITION?

WOULD YOU RATHER...

BE AN INTERNET SENSATION FROM DOING SOMETHING NERDY

- OR -

BE AN INTERNET SENSATION FROM DOING SOMETHING EMBARRASSING?

BRUSH YOUR TEETH USING A BAR OF SOAP
- OR -
BRUSH YOUR TEETH USING TWO-MONTH-OLD MILK?

WOULD YOU RATHER...

NOT HAVE TOILET PAPER WHILE YOU'RE ON THE TOILET SEAT

- OR -

NOT HAVE WATER TO WASH YOUR HANDS WITH AFTERWARD?

BE EATEN BY YOUR DOG

- OR -

HAVE YOUR DIARY READ OUT IN PUBLIC?

WOULD YOU RATHER...

FOLD ALL THE CLOTHES

- OR -

WASH ALL THE DIRTY CLOTHES?

HAVE A SMALL ZIT THAT WON'T GO AWAY

- OR -

HAVE A MASSIVE ZIT THAT WILL POP?

WOULD YOU RATHER...

SLEEP BESIDE A SKUNK

- OR -

SLEEP BESIDE A PIG?

BE IN THE DEBATE CLUB

- OR -

WATCH A DEBATE?

WOULD YOU RATHER...

BE IN YOUR FAVORITE VIDEO GAME

- *OR* -

BE IN YOUR FAVORITE CARTOON?

GO TO A DANCE WITH SOMEONE WHO HAS
BODY ODOR
- *OR* -
GO TO A DANCE WITH SOMEONE WHO HAS
BAD BREATH?

WOULD YOU RATHER...

MEET A DONKEY THAT TALKS

- OR -

MEET A DONKEY THAT WALKS ON TWO LEGS?

BE A BRAIN SURGEON

- OR -

BE A SCIENTIST?

WOULD YOU RATHER...

HAVE THE ABILITY TO TALK TO ANIMALS

- *OR* -

BE ABLE TO HEAR ANIMALS TALK?

NEVER GET TO EAT DONUTS FOR THE REST OF YOUR LIFE

- *OR* -

EAT ONLY DONUTS FOR AN ENTIRE WEEK?

WOULD YOU RATHER...

BE MUCH SHORTER

- *OR* -

BE MUCH TALLER?

DROP YOUR NEW PHONE DOWN TO THE
TOILET
- *OR* -
DROP YOUR CHARM BRACELET DOWN THE
SINK?

WOULD YOU RATHER...

HAVE YOUR LEG STUCK IN THE TOILET BOWL

- OR -

HAVE YOUR HANDS STUCK IN THE TOILET BOWL?

SEE A FUNNY VIDEO OF YOUR PARENTS ONLINE

- OR -

SEE A FUNNY VIDEO OF A CLOSE FRIEND ONLINE?

WOULD YOU RATHER...

BE VERY UNPOPULAR

- OR -

BE SUPER POPULAR AND BE STALKED BY PAPARAZZI ALL THE TIME?

LOSE YOUR FAVORITE TOY

- OR -

LOSE ALL YOUR SAVINGS?

WOULD YOU RATHER...

EAT 1 SPIDER

- *OR* -

A WHOLE BOWL OF WORMS?

WATCH TV IN BED ALONE

- *OR* -

WATCH TV ON THE COUCH WITH YOUR

FAMILY?

WOULD YOU RATHER...

HAVE TWO REALLY SHORT LEGS

- OR -

HAVE ONE LEG SHORTER THAN THE OTHER?

BE ABLE TO DRAW AMAZINGLY WELL

- OR -

BE ABLE TO SING REALLY, REALLY WELL?

WOULD YOU RATHER...

A GO TO COSTUME PARTY

- OR -

TO A TEA PARTY?

HAVE AN AUNT THAT PATS YOUR HEAD A LOT
- OR -
HAVE AN AUNT THAT PULLS YOUR CHEEKS
A LOT?

WOULD YOU RATHER...

BE BITTEN BY A MOSQUITO 10 TIMES

- OR -

BE STUNG BY A BEE 1 TIME?

THROW UP ON YOUR CRUSH

- OR -

THROW UP ON YOUR BEST FRIEND?

WOULD YOU RATHER...

LOOK LIKE AN OLD PERSON

- *OR* -

SOUND LIKE AN OLD PERSON?

SWIM IN ICE-COLD WATER

- *OR* -

SWIM IN A POOL OF HOT WATER?

WOULD YOU RATHER...

GET A FREE PLANE TICKET

- OR -

GET A FREE BOAT CRUISE?

BE ABLE RUN ON WATER

- OR -

BE ABLE TO BREATHE UNDERWATER?

WOULD YOU RATHER...

NEVER EAT FAST FOOD AGAIN

- *OR* -

EAT FAST FOOD FOR EVERY SINGLE MEAL FOR THE REST OF YOUR LIFE?

BE PRANKED WITHH A FAKE BUG

- *OR* -

BE PRANKED WITH A FAKE RAT?

WOULD YOU RATHER...

STOP DRINKING ANYTHING COLD ALTOGETHER

- OR -

GET A BRAIN FREEZE EVERY TIME YOU DRANK SOMETHING COLD?

SEND A PRANK TEXT

- OR -

DO A PRANK PHONE CALL?

WOULD YOU RATHER...

SHOWER WITH HOT WATER

- OR -

SHOWER WITH COLD WATER?

BE UNABLE TO CELEBRATE HALLOWEEN

- OR -

BE UNABLE TO CELEBRATE CHRISTMAS?

WOULD YOU RATHER...

FIND LOTS OF EASTER EGGS

- OR -

MEET THE EASTER BUNNY?

HAVE TO SING EVERY TIME YOU HEARD
A SONG

- OR -

HAVE TO DANCE EVERY TIME YOU HEARD A
SONG?

WOULD YOU RATHER...

BE IN A HOUSE FILLED WITH CANDY

- *OR* -

BE IN A HOUSE FILLED WITH MARSHMALLOWS?

GO SKYDIVING
- *OR* -
GO BUNGEE JUMPING?

WOULD YOU RATHER...

HAVE SUPER STRENGTH

- OR -

HAVE SUPER SPEED?

LIVE IN THE SKY PERMANENTLY

- OR -

UNDERWATER PERMANENTLY?

WOULD YOU RATHER...

NEVER HAVE CANDY, EVER AGAIN

- OR -

TO ONLY EAT CANDY FOR THE REST OF YOUR LIFE?

BE STUCK IN A TOILET BECAUSE THE TOILET DOOR WON'T OPEN

- OR -

BE STUCK IN A TOILET BECAUSE YOUR POOP WON'T FLUSH?

WOULD YOU RATHER...

GO WITH MOM TO WORK

- *OR* -

HAVE YOUR MOM STAY AT HOME ALL DAY?

BECOME THE SIZE OF A WHALE

- *OR* -

BE SHRUNK DOWN TO THE SIZE OF A BUG?

WOULD YOU RATHER...

WEAR ANY CLOTHING OF YOUR CHOICE TO SCHOOL

- OR -

WEAR YOUR SCHOOL UNIFORM ALL THE TIME?

TELEPORT TO THE SURFACE OF THE MOON
- OR -
TO THE BOTTOM OF THE OCEAN?

CPSIA information can be obtained
at www.ICGtesting.com
Printed in the USA
LVHW050245051121
702512LV00005B/124

9 781989 626184